# ECE KARADAG

# Lachrymose

*First edition*

*Cover art by John Everett Millais*

*This book was professionally typeset on Reedsy.*
*Find out more at reedsy.com*

*My love, this is for you...*

"You never know what is enough unless you know what is more than enough."

William Blake, The Marriage of Heaven and Hell.

# Contents

## III    Songs of Love and Despair

# Acknowledgement

First of all, I would like to thank my dear friend Kudret Seher Aksu, who I love very much and who is more than a sister.

Afterwards, my sincere thanks to my beloved family, to whom I owe every breath I take. I wouldn't exist without you, and none of these lines would perhaps ever have been written, none of these feelings would ever have happened.

Then I would love to send my sincere thanks to my beloved professors who's more than a professor, they always supported me and they always believed that I could achieve good things.

Lastly, you, my dear readers, I would like to express my endless thanks to you. Because if it weren't for you, no one would understand me.

With my most sincere and deepest respect and love,

*-Ece.*

# Content Warnings

This book contains material that can be triggering for some audiences, like depression, mention of wounds, physical violence, mental violence, death, grief and mention of self-harm.

# I

# A Thousand and One Nights of Sadness or Prologue

*For the girl I used to be...*

# The Manifesto of a Hopeless Lover or Prologue

*Being disliked,* it was the *sickness* of our century,
*Unrequited love,* it was the greatest *disaster* of our world,
And I've been living through this disaster
Because of a *relentless man.*

O, never! I will not, I will not unbosom your name,
But you and your legacy will
always live in my broken heart.
O, never! Never ever!

*Being loved,* it was the *sickness* of our century,
*Falling in love,* it was the greatest *disaster* of our world,
And I've been living through this disaster
Because of an *unmerciful man.*

# One More Chance to Love You Again

My darling, owner of my moody soul,
owner of my reckless heart.
Hold my hands and take me up,
Because I got tired of being at the bottom.

Take me up, and I'll take you to my Garden of Eden,
Let me give you the thornless roses of my heart.

Please don't refuse them
Please my darling, please give me one more chance to love you again.
Please darling, give me one more chance to die for you again.

# A Night When My Eternal Hopes Faded

I loved you on a night
when my eternal hopes faded,
My eyes met with your eyes,
And I start to blaze
with an eternal hope again.

I loved you at a moment
when an endless night
was mixed with numbered days,
I loved you, your flaws
And your sins unconditionally.

You were a war that broke out inside me,
And I was a weak soldier with the plague.
I resisted you endless times,
but you knocked me down
in a single move.

I loved you on a night
when my eternal hopes faded,
My eyes met with your eyes,
And I start to blaze
with an eternal hope again.

LACHRYMOSE

My mother is crying by my grave and
She was wondering why I died suddenly,
But she doesn't know
the ruins of that war that
Still burns inside me.

Cleanse me from this sea of sin,
Cleanse the soul of that
frightened child still
living inside of me.
O, Holy Mother! Hear me!
O, Holy Mother, I know you're still there!

# Ophelia

I

We are all the *Ophelia* of our own story,
Some of us ends their lives like *her*.
Some of us are trying to hold on to life,
just like *"us"* despite all the hopelessness.

I was Ophelia of my own story,
But I am sinking to the bottom,
just as her dead body.
Just please, please help me!

We are all the *Ophelia* of our own story,
Some of us ends their lives like *her*.
Some of us are trying to hold on to life,
just like *"us"* despite all the hopelessness.
But right now, we're all dying just like *her*.

II

Please don't put *black roses* on our grave, o, never!
Give us *white lilies* from the Garden of Holy Mary.
Symbolise our *purity* and the *virginity* of our holy mother!
Please don't put black roses on our grave, o, never!

Bury us where the *willow trees* will protect us.
Remember us with *pansies*
like as you remember Ophelia.
But never put *buttercups* on our graves
like the one you put on Ophelia's grave.


III


Why did you immortalise her pain
while making this painting, Sir?
Why did you make this painting and
condemn her to die and suffer once again?


O, Ophelia! My beloved Ophelia!
I can hear the scream of your tears!
Give me a chance, give me a chance
to heal your wounds
My beloved Ophelia!


Why did you have to be so sad, my beloved Ophelia?
Why did I have to be so relentless, my beloved Ophelia?
Give me a chance, give me a chance
to heal your wounds
My beloved Ophelia!

# Tears of Today

I wiped all the tears that I shed for today,
Can you hear the helpless bawls of my tears?
It was a rainy and stormy Wednesday
when I presented my heart to you on a salver.

When lightning pierces the delicate hymen of the sky,
You pierce my heart with great pleasure with your sharp dagger.
I just cry and cry,
I'm begging you, don't go. Please.

I'm afraid of lightning, you know.
Cover me up with your big hands
and tell me how much you love me,
Make me believe this lie, darling.

# Scratched Vinyls

His voice was like a scratched vinyl,
was sincere, but something was preventing him
from presenting his sincerity to me,
It kept my heart from his sincerity.
The only thing that kept him and
his memories alive was this vinyl.
And now, I am losing it,
just like I was losing him.

# To My Family or The First Chapter of My Life

I owe you all the breaths I take,
I owe you all the dreams
I have ever dreamed,
Long story short,
I owe you, my life.
If it weren't for you, maybe
I would never have left a mark
on this world.
Maybe if it wasn't for you,
God I don't even want to think!

Counting every step I take,
Thanking God for every breath I take,
My family who are happy with me
for every success I have achieved,
God bless you!
God never separate you from me!
I believe that we will
achieve more happiness
and achieve new
successes together.
I will always be yours.

Your daughter who will
always be your one and only…

12

# Gate of Eden

Take my breath away first,
then take my heart last.
At the end,
We met near the coast.

The wind was fondling my hair,
I whispered your name slowly
with a deep pleasure
to the air.

You hold my tiny hand
with your giant heart
without agape
and sympathy.

My heart met with
your eternal compassion
in the gate of Eden.

# Letters from Mr. Nobody

I got several letters from Mr. Nobody,
The letters were so heavy that
my heart couldn't take it.
The words smelled of love, suicide and
deep grief.

The lines were written with the
blood of Mr. Nobody's hopes flowing,
Every word was crying like
it was at the funeral,
At the funeral of a man in love.

# Unfinished Poems, Unwritten Lines

My soul feeds on your memories,
my soul feeds on your love.
My blind eyes revives only bu your appearance,
But without you, I will not survive,
just like my eternal soul.
All that's left was my lost hope
and my lost love for you.
I tried to heal the wounds
you opened in my heart,
but my love for you was
getting in the way.
Help me heal,
for the sake of which
I will give my soul.
I beg you,
don't kill me one more time,
have pity on me.

# II

# Blanched Pages, Unsent Postcard

*For the girl I am now...*

# Melody of a Broken Heart

Close your eyes and dream,
Feel every melody of your heart.
Let the sunshine gleam,
Who said it's that really hard?

Sing until the mornings do us part,
Hold my heart and take it to your ear
And listen to the melody of *a* broken heart.
Listen to the melody of *my* broken heart.

I was like a bird that lost its voice,
I spread my wings and soared in the sky,
I know I have no other choice.
Because nobody asked me *why*.

You asked me to show my *gratitude* towards you,
And I brought you hydrangeas abloom.
I looked into your stinging blue eyes.
I felt you to my bones, dearest gloom.

Sing until the mornings do us part,
Hold my heart and take it to your ear
And listen to the melody of *a* broken heart.
Listen to the melody of *my* broken heart.

# Poem for Him

i opened the lights of mine own weakened heart,
to bid you,
mankind is not immortal
not perfect.

storms hit the fertile earth
with might and main.
earth wast begging to storms
don't did hurt mine own crops.
anon doomsday shall cometh
and that gent shall greets us coldly.
Supreme being shall weight our sins
and valorous deeds.
and then that gentleman shall sends us
to the deepest part of the hell.

nobody is sinless, nobody is perfect, except you.
Closed thy eyes, mine own love,
and bid me,
Took a deep breath and
asked
don't you loved me?

# King of the Bullet

He was the King of Bullet,
He was very cruel more than anyone.
His fingers were fat, cheeks were scarlet,
Needs to encolour his cheeks with the blood of someone.
We don't want you, You glorious king!
Drifted along the bayou,
Take out that dignified ring!
Go to Hell, go to Hell!
Get out of here, you Demon!
Your end is not well,
Okay you are not our eudemon!
On the last floor of Purgatory,
The results were unsatisfactory.

# Conqueror of Hell


He was the Conqueror of Hell,
Be redempt with the blood of the innocent!
The Ark of Hell's sail was swell.
We will all rise before the crescent.
Revive, all you glorious sinful souls, revive!
Release the Cerberus, release the Cerberus!
There is no way to survive.
Hell smells like a citrus.
The innocents were in pain,
They lost their personalities in the conquest of endless Hell,
Everything was in vain.
Farewell my beautiful homeland, farewell!
It was slipping from our palms,
The Ark of Hell was filling with halms.

# Purgatory of Innocent Souls

Redempt me with your endless power,
My heart is a cauldron and you are the elixir in it.
All the innocent souls were sitting in the bower.
We innocent souls cannot do without it.
Innocent souls were alone in Purgatory What did we have but to confess?
Everyone would write their own history,
So we can only profess.
A white dove descends on us slowly,
Greet the innocent with great joy.
The demon loved all the souls hollowly,
But he will destroy
With the supreme power of Lucifer,
And everyone would suffer.

# The Ninth Circle of Hell or the Treachery

An intense cold greets you with a satisfaction,
I know you want to escape from here, my dear.
All you have to do is redemption,
Without any tension or fear.
No one can help you, you cannot escape.
Welcome to the Ninth Circle of Hell,
You shouldn't eat the treachery's grape.
Listen to the loud voice of the Holy Bell!
It's a cold place with shouts and cries,
Cry my beautiful, cry.
This is the centre of the shattered skies.
They die under the pieces of the sky. The frozen bloods drips to the ground,
The Ninth Circle of Hell is very profound.

# Hell-hounds in the Mortal World

There are millions of hell-hounds in the mortal world,
Those gents shall consume mortals with pleasure.
those gents swirled, those gents swirled…
foolishness is their greatest treasure.
drive the sharp dagger into the hearts of mortals,
Kill 'em, did beat 'em,
don't allow 'em wend out through the portals.
Help me to kill 'em, mine own dearest Jem!
snakes knows the sooth, snakes knows the sooth!
take thy steps well,
or those gents shall take hence thy youth!
the mortal world shall hath fallen,
the mortal world shall hath fallen!
Be obstinate to exterminate,
but thy limits art determinate.

# For Luna

Today is Sunday,
Our paths will cross where you open your eyes
to this cruel world.

I took you in my arms for the first time.
I can tell by your black fur that you are a strong cat.
I can tell by its white fur that you are a pure cat.
But all I know is you're my *only* one.

I cannot express my gratitude
and love for you in these powerless words.
I will always be your mother,
and I will be honoured to be your mother.

# A Whimp

Blood flows with most wondrous lust over the fertile land,
bid me ladybird what can i do for you?
give me your tiny hand,
thou art the most wondrous sinner, i knew.
Hold mine own hands lest i kick the bucket,
what's thy purpose, you ghoul?
we did lie under the endless sky.
Her dress is as bright as her innocent soul!
Screams all the innocent,
i don't want to kick the bucket, you forgive me!
for the first time, i see you magnificent,
mine own only sin wast that gent.
what were you doing, you simp,
thou art the only whimp!

# A Poem for My Rosy-Cheeked Gentleman

A rosy-cheeked gentleman appeared on the horizon of hell,
He kissed my eyes from afar with great happiness and love.
Tell me darling, for whom did you take your life?
Tell me darling, for whom did you take my life?
Your shining tears run down your Rosy-cheeks,
Tell me what makes you cry darling.
Tell me the reason so I can bind your wounds tighter.
Let my love heal you, darling.
Let my love heal all of your wounds.

# Back Flowing River of Heaven

From the virgin River of Heaven,
the waters flowed backwards.
At that moment,
I understood that the Devil has come.
His red lips made me want to kiss passionately.
In the Garden of Eden, we were two lusty angels.
I didn't know he was the Devil.
I was in love with a fallen angel.
Forgive me, Lord, for my greatest sin.
Forgive me Lord, forgive me!
Curse every breath I take, O great Lord!
Curse every step I take, every word I say!
But do not curse my love for him, great Lord!

# When Life Hurts You

*Tom Odell this poem is for you!*

When life hurts you wipe
your tears and smile,
Smile with your whole being,
with great love to this damn world!

When life hurts you,
unite the broken pieces of
your heart
with great love!

You deserve to be loved
and exalted,
not to be sad!

Wipe your tears
and look at the sky!
Shout out all your gratitude
for existing in this world!

# When the Flames Go Out

When the flames go out,
the whole world slowly cools down
with the pain of grief.

Bodies cool down
and die, those in the
grip of death.

Tell me, if there is no fire,
how will this human being
get warm, how will he exist?
How he gets rid of painful mourning,
grief and sorrow?

How will we survive
without this fire?
How then will we find
the lost peace?
How will we reach that
eternal existence and peace?

# Chiromancy

Tell me what you see, *palmister*.
What will happen to me?
Am I going to die because of this poisonous arrow of *love*?
I'm trapped in the prison of my misfortune,
Tell me what will happen to me.
Will I lose myself like I lost him?
What do you see in my hand?
You can't see it because you can't look carefully.
You are afraid because I will die or suffer.
Tell me what you see, *palmister*.
What will happen to me?
Tell me what you see.

# The Gold Medallion


Pearls representing your
glorious face hanging from
my gold medallion
which attached to my glorious heart,
and those dried red rose petals
that set hearts ablaze…

Loving you is like the
infatuation of a butterfly with
a life span of one day
for a raven that lives for more than a century.

If falling in love is a sin,
I am the greatest sinner
and the greatest lover.

# They were Kissing the Graves of Their Mothers

I'm crying but you can't see
I'm sorry but you can't see.
I kneel before you
and beg you to forgive me,
but you don't see, mommy!
You can't see, you can't see!
I miss you with
every breath I take, mommy!

No, mommy, don't go,
don't leave me alone
in this cruel world.
Mommy, mommy!
I'm losing my mind, you're gone,
You're gone, I lost my mind.

# Can You Hear the Melody of my Sorrow?

Can you hear the melody of my sorrow?
What does he want to shout?
What does he want to reveal?
Or are you just listening, mister?
Please answer my question,
I am not a wicked person!
I'm just a lonely and helpless woman in this
In this cruel and dreary world.
Don't, don't, mister!
Please don't go,
It won't be quiet if you go!
Please help me silence him!
Please, sir.
Do not be so cruel as him.
Do not hesitate to help me,
help me, mister! I'm drowning,
I am in pain.
I'm dying, mister!
He is my killer.
But you are the one who let him kill, mister.

# Rain of Love

Behold the sky float in my heart,
My heart whispers you to
the sky with great desire,
Be mine, be mine,
be the spring of my pain,
be the cure of my pain.

Take my hands and rule them,
Rule them as if they need you.
Caress my hair, stroke it as they need it.
But never leave me in these deep thoughts.

We dance in the pouring rain.
You were looking at her while I was looking at you with love.
While I'm getting wet under the rain of love
and falling in love with you,
You were falling in love with her.
You wanted her with all your heart,
I wanted you with all my heart.

# Extinguished Incenses

What is it that we call life?
As weak as extinguished incense,
But it's as strong as a flame that stirs it.
The smoke of incense dances
in the sky with the oxygen.
Maybe this is the last dance of
the incense smoke.
Take my hands and
tell me which of us is weaker,
The smoke of the
dying incense or me?

# III

# Songs of Love and Despair

*For the girl I'll be in the future...*

# When The Goldfinch Died

Everyone woke up today
with the sound of a gun,
But nobody saw the
goldfinch writhing in pain.

When the goldfinch died,
Mother Nature died,
The birds drowned
in deep mourning.
And mankind died.

The groan of the goldfinch
surrounded her in pain,
As she takes her last breath,
Mankind watched her die
with a deep pleasure.

# Ode to Apollo

Oh, Apollo!
You run your long and thin
fingers over the strings of your lyre,
There's a big satyr
running around.
He was writing something
in his leather notebook.

Laurel wreath on your head,
You wish her
with all your heart.

She ran away from you
until she turned into a tree.
Do not curse me, my God,
Truth hurts,
Just like she hurts you.

# The Sudden Death of Igor Igorevich

Igor Igorevich had sworn
he would never do it again.
But his pure heart followed
the devil.

He killed the innocents
with all his grudge,
He killed without blinking an eye,
St. Petersburg bathed
in the blood of the innocents.

Whereas his heart was pure,
It was just like
his mother's milk.
Sinless and just as pure.
Everything was good for him
until that day.
It would never be
the same again.

# Broken Tears, Broken Hiccups

I collected the tears
running down my cheeks,
I gulped all
the broken hiccups in me.

I hid my tears in
a fragile bell jar,
I can't stop,
Tears running down
my cheeks
and my hiccups pouring
from my lips.

# Take my hand first, then destroy me

Take my hand first,
then destroy me.
Never pity to
my sinful soul.

I was born
in darkness,
I will die
in darkness.

Take my hand first,
then destroy me.
Never pity to
my sinful soul.

Stick your dagger
to my chest,
Let the blood gush
into the skies.

Let me die once more in peace
Don't tell me how to die
Believe me,
This death is not my first death.

# To Beatrice

Tell me what's on your mind,
darling,
Say you don't love me,
Say you don't owe me.

Confess all the truth with
your delicate mouth,
With the meticulousness of your heart,
break my heart again.

But never lie to me, darling,
Lies hurt,
disgusts people from themselves
However, the world is
built on lies.

Tell me, Beatrice,
Tell me the hardest truths
of hardest life.
Hurt me again like you used to,
No pain could bring me this much pleasure.

# What were the foxes wandering inside my head telling me?

I was lonely, so lonely,
My soul was empty like a bottomless hole.
Now I have a heart tired like a minute vane
Tired of moving.

The foxes wandering inside my head,
It was preventing me from loving you.
They knew everything all the truths.
What were the foxes wandering inside
my head telling me?

# Ode to my family

I owe you all the breaths I take,
I owe you all the dreams I have ever dreamed,
Long story short, I owe you, my life.
If it weren't for you, maybe
I would never have left a mark on this world.
Maybe if it wasn't for you, God I don't even want to think!

Counting every step I take,
Thanking God for every breath I take,
My family who are happy with me for every success I have achieved,
God bless you!
God never separate you from me!
I believe that we will achieve more happiness
and achieve new successes together.
I will always be yours.

# I Loved a Man

i loved a man,
whose soul smells like
an old bookstore.
his dimple welcomes us
with a deep pleasure.
the wisdom is his
greatest treasure.

nobody persuades me,
i keep pace with chorus.
nobody persuades me,
i got with the times.

an old,
wise soul,
hates this,
age of ignorance,
with full of supercilious people.

# Cherry Wines

broken goblets,
hearts screaming in pain.
blood bleeding pens,
weeping papers.

let's get drunk together tonight,
bless us dionysus
with a shining wreath on your head.
offer us your best cherry wines.

we made offers, we sacrificed
all living things for you,
o great dionysus!
bless us dionysus
with a shining wreath on your head.
offer us your best cherry wines.

# Eternal Souls in the Mortal World

my hair strands between fingers
you were kissing me
until you were out of breath
what's going on in your head?
we were like eternal
souls in the mortal world.

kiss me first, then kill me
we have no memory left behind
only my soul was
flying in the sky

you were looking in astonishment
as I lustfully look at you.
do not be afraid,
the dead will not hurt you.
the eternal spirits of the mortal
world will never hurt you.

# i took him to heaven (stanzas one & two)

he asked me to take him somewhere,
and i took him to heaven.
i dug abandoned graves,
to find peace in eternity.

and a dove appeared,
at the gate of infinity.
there is only one way
to escape from reality.

# master of sorrow

i was touching his calloused soul,
with my eternal hopes.
can anybody hear me?
my scream awakes all of the dead souls.

except prejudiced souls,
and minds.
my scream echoed,
and trees flapped with nature's rhythm.

jeremiah, oh jeremiah,
hear my dolefully jeremiads, groaning with pain.
begging you, i believe,
i will revive your dead soul.

there is a man,
praying to god, for all blessings.
but there's no hearer,
in this world.

you are the master of sorrow,
in my world.
but there is just a remedy.
your believing to me wholeheartedly.

# i took him to heaven (stanzas three & four)

i brought flowers from the garden of innocence,
but he refused to get the flowers,
from his fallen angel.
then i collapsed.

being able to love a person,
requires accepting him in everything.
with his sins, his endless tears,
sometimes it is necessary to give him your heart.

# to her monsieur

i dare not to send,
all the love letters i wrote,
i am afraid,
because my words can kill him.

words, oh words,
words can kill people.
because words are like a sharp knife,
the sharp knife of unrequited love.

# autumn breeze

his smile is like autumn
it was as cold as the breeze.
his gaze is as dreamy as
a summer night.

memories are on fire
was burning in the stove
the traces he left wipe away
they were going one by one.

love me first, kiss me later
like you will never leave,
hold me in your arms
never love me again.

# Burning tears

Another woman's breaking
Heart is falling down
Pain and gloom are eructing
Passion flames to my face.

He stole away my vile heart
With his precious eyes
No more suffer
Forgive me Lucifer
Because I will no longer obey you.

# first untitled poem

whispered azrael,
angel of the bitter death,
he asked,
what's my only wish.
i whispered to air,
he touched my hair.
tell me little one, tell me what is your only wish.
die, i want to die azrael.
but he didn't take my life,
he said i was too innocent to die.
too innocent.

i saw a dried blood stain,
on the white marble.
dried blood stain of
my innocence.
how many more times my heart broke,
i did not count.
actually,
how much more could a broken heart break?
how could someone with a hard heart still feel the pain?
from the cup of love
how many times did these mortals drink the bitter poison?

we were the broken hearts in broken goblets.
and we all lose our strength.
we lose the blood that we draw strength from,
of the cracked glasses,
it flows, the blood we pump.


a ship
i am the last traveler.
but i got no waving,
who cries behind me.
we go alone,
wherever we go.

# melody of icarus

don't fly too close
to the sun
with melting wings.
drowns in time,
that deep, abysmal water.

flies insoluble,
as if he would never drown
as if he was not going to give
his life with his hands.
they had admonished him:
don't fly too close
to the sun
with melting wings.

# the ballad of ethereal queen

a crown made of flower could only
make a person so beautiful.
tell me, tell me
what is your secret?


the infinitely beautiful queen living in
the sparkling palace of the fairies,
tell me, tell me
what is your secret?

# second untitled poem

i, the greatest sinner,
i would never deny that i liked you.
the sweet pain of my heart, the sweet pain of my heart,
i was born with your love; i will die with your love.

i can't tell my love to you, darling,
because no words
enough to tell you
not powerful and honourable.
i left my mind with all of me
i left my mother and father behind me.
if you see what i am in
i am a wandering madman with an empty head.

i'm not ashamed of my love for you,
speaking.
i'm telling you
like a butterfly loves a raven,
i love you.

no, you for me
more than a lover.
to call it love, it will be less,
it's not love either.

SECOND UNTITLED POEM

don't tell, don't tell,
you are in love with him.
i can't take it any longer
to the pain and the inability to receive
the reward of my love and love.

do not be spoiled honey.
come on tell me
what is ours?
what are these feelings i feel for you?
really, what is this pain?

# the waves

kissing under the endless sun
two couples who *madly*
love each other.
they were screaming while
kissing their *love* lustfully.

the waves were hitting
the slopes of the cliffs,
a young girl was preparing
to jump off a cliff
to embrace the raging waves.

# chamomile tea

*pour my chamomile tea fondly,*
*kiss the earth, thank to mother nature.*
*get your cup, and brew some*
*love from chamomiles.*

*loves me,*
*loves me not.*
*isn't everything like this, anyway?*

*in this short time,*
*which has black and white keys,*
*makes different sounds from each of them.*
*some people make love accompanying that voices,*
*in all the rhythms.*
*some people cry, with the sorrow of those rhythms.*

*kiss me slowly, kiss and whisper*
*whisper that you love me,*
*whisper that you owe me.*

# cafuné

there are billions of letters
i dare not send you.
my words can hurt you,
because my words are
my armed guards.

when i run my fingers through your hair,
i forgot how much i love you,
i whispered my secrets
to the air.

a flower bloomed in the middle of my heart
can hurt so much.

# the grave digger


i am the grave digger.
digging all of the desperate bodies,
who's singing along to the death song,
with azrael.


bodies were suffused with,
the colours of a salamander skin.
black and yellow,
every inch smell,
like a new-born baby.


i grieved,
i grieved because of,
carrying mortal's all of the sins on my back,
then i collapsed.

# dreamers

dagger was piercing my chest very madly,
my crimson blood and my life.
what's this war for?
for who?

roses were bleeding,
violets were crying.
dreamers cannot stop themselves,
while searching their dreams.

# august dream

chrysanthemums danced to the
chirping of fireflies
with great passion.
that was the
august dream in them.


we were swinging
light wind was blowing
the voices of shouting children
interrupting our conversation


you wish that august would never end
but you didn't know
every good thing has an end
this is like other memories
the memory would be
immortalized in our memory box.

# ode to lucifer

*can you hear my*
*desperate screams*
*from the deepest level of*
*inferno?*

*can you hear my*
*desperate screams?*
*i was an angel*
*like them.*

*why did they*
*shut me out of heaven?*
*is it for telling*
*people to sin?*

*mama, papa,*
*are you there?*
*can you hear my*
*desperate screams?*
*from the deepest level of*
*inferno?*

# champagne stains

pop up champagne and
pour into my golden goblet.
let's get drunk tonight,
and hit the bottom of
our love like all lovers.

let's get drunk tonight,
and kiss forever
like it will never end.

let's get drunk tonight,
and make love with you
every night with
a great desire.

let's get drunk tonight,
and kill the childish soul in us.
let's get drunk tonight,
let's get drunk tonight.
let's…

# forbidden faces

they see, you see the
forbidden faces of our
dark, bleak century.
they were staring us
desperately.

that cold february night
slowly as the god lowered
the snow from the sky
the wind is blowing hard
help me, help me
help me to find forbidden faces
of our dark, bleak century.

# Mama, Pt. 1

Why does it have to be like this?
Why do you have
to be the one to suffer
while I suffer?
Don't mama, don't mama.

Do not leave me
in the clutches of
this cruel world.
Don't leave me
in this darkness mama,
I'm afraid.

I was swinging you
on the swing, suddenly
the rope broke and
I buried you in the ground.
No, no, don't leave me, mama!

# Mama, Pt. 2

Why are your hands cold, mama?
The sun embraces us warmly.
Why can't I feel your love, mama?
Wrap me in your arms
like the sun,
with your love that
will warm me.

Why are you afraid, mama?
Are you afraid of me,
Or is it my deep love for you?
Tell me, mama.

# Healing the wounded heart

Embrace my wounded heart
with all your sincerity,
Kiss my red lips
where the taste of
innocence will spread.

But never tell me
how much you love me,
Because this can
hurt me the most!

With your big hand,
hold my tiny hand
with your
great tenderness.

While the
autumn breeze blows
between us,
Your breath
warms my whole body.

Hear my prayers and pleas!
My cries, my cries of pain...

Please remember me,
Please don't pity me.

# Mama, Pt. 3

Why can't I feel your love, mama?
Are you afraid?
I didn't want to hurt you.

Take my hand,
let's get out of here.
Maybe you will
like me there.
Maybe I will see the
value I deserve there.

# Losing a loved one

Losing a person you
owe your breath to,
Losing a person to whom
you owe every step you take,
Is worse than death.

Now I realize how happy
we were in the past,
How peaceful we used to be,
how quiet and painful it is now.

I miss you,
I am filled with
longing to the bone.
*Please, come back.*
*Please, come back.*

# The Bible of Phœbus

Our destiny was written
in the Bible of Phœbus,
Hope and Love beheaded all
of the malignancy with
a sharp axe.

She was picking
the dead lilies
that sprouted in the
middle of my broken heart.

# what was the colour of my lonely soul?

i am holding the
colour of your
breath in my palms,
which is crimson red.

i was walking
in your shade
on a warm
summer evening.

you were breathing
the cold into my palms
to warm me but
i was getting colder.

what was the colour
of our love
in those black and
white photos?

what was the colour
of your lovely soul?

what was the colour

WHAT WAS THE COLOUR OF MY LONELY SOUL?

of my lonely soul?

# what is the name of the eternal love?

tell me what is the
name of the eternal
love in me
towards you.

tell me what color
is the skin color of
your compassion that
i hold in my hands.

i fell in love with
you under the candlelight,
how was the taste
of Turkish delight?

in the middle of the night
your smile rose like a sun.

# bright light of eternal love

the sky roars with the
flapping of wings of
the fallen angels.

one touch illuminates
heaven with the
fire of hell.

all eyes are blinded by
the bright light of his
impossible and
eternal love.

# Immortalising Stars

One night I gathered the bright stars
in the black sky.
I wanted to immortalise the stars,
Tell me, tell me, why.

Glitters of stars sticking to my hand,
Cast a spell with that wand.
But don't give up, my love,
Sooner or later
my hands will be in your hands.

# With my warmest wishes

I send my warmest wishes
to you on this beautiful day,
I embrace you all with
the most sincere sincerity.

You are not alone, my friends.
You will never be alone.
I embrace you with
all my love and warmth.

Sometimes you feel helpless
and sometimes lonely,

But I am with you.
Never be afraid
to be alone.
'Cause you will
never be alone.

# Peculiar Sensations Society

I didn't count how many cups of coffee I drank today,
But I couldn't forget you.
I couldn't forget you
And your betrayal.

It was a heartbreaking melody
that you hummed,
But I could not feel the bitterness in my heart,
Maybe it's because I'm heartless.

# Lady or A Requiem to My Lady

Oh my Lady, my beautiful
Golden haired Lady!
Another year passes without you,
We only desire, your great love and
Beautiful smile.

Wipe those tears and look up to sky,
And smile at us.
God will descend as a
Dove and smile back at you.

You gave us eternity,
In numbered days.
We are grateful to you,
Your supreme love and
Your divine power.
Always with you,
In your precious heart.

# Ode to My Tooth Fairy

Oh my dear Tooth Fairy,
Tell me where are my pearls,
where have you hidden them,
under the fertile soil of what mysterious garden?

Tell me my Tooth Fairy,
Where are my golds?
Where did you hide them?
Or did you put it in the safest place,
on my mother's chest?

Oh my dear Tooth Fairy,
Where are you?
I need you in these years, in this lifetime.
Come and save me from this famine.
Let's fertilize every soil together.

# A Cup of Coffee as a Moody Soul

A dark coffee carefully prepared
for you with its carefully roasted beans.
Sir, would you like a cup of coffee
as dark as your moody soul?

Sir, would you like a cup of coffee
as dark as your moody soul?
As terrifying and dreadful as a ghoul,
Tell me who owns my gullible soul?

# My Love Monsieur Rouquin

Do not worry my love,
My love is eternal
And my love can't hurt you.
Trust me,
My Love Monsieur Rouquin.

I saw the light of the torch in your heart.
He lights up the darkness with full truth.
I have listened to the song of your wounded heart.
They sing with deep sadness.

# Saint R.

Today I buried my childhood and my purity,
to the dark, marble grave.
Everybody think I can't revive,
But I don't have power to
prove them they're wrong.

Saint R., Saint R.
I lost my way,
Be my compass, show me,
show me where shall I go.

Birds were singing a hymn,
Daisies were dropping their leaves.
Humanity were losing his
purity.

# Broken, delicate heart

I was holding your broken, delicate heart,
I didn't know it would be this hard.
I didn't know that loving you and forgetting
you would be so hard and so painful.

I'm afraid, afraid of everything,
I'm afraid because you exist,
Cruel and selfish.
I hate you, but don't leave me,
I am a weak-winged dove.

# IV

# Extinct Memories or Family Portraits

*for everyone in my family*

# Loving Someone Without Knowing



How can I describe the *love*?
It was easy to describe what is love but
the hardest thing is describing the
loving someone you haven't met.
And I always loved you like this, Grandpa.

I never hold your hands
with my tiny soul.
I never smiled or giggled with you.
And I never felt your
deepest care or love for me.

But I always believed in one thing,
I always see your shadow and
felt your soul with me.
And I believed only one thing
which is you are still with me.
You left this world too early,
But not for me, you are still in this world
and playing hide and seek with us.

I believe we will meet someday in Heaven,
And I believe,
I will find where you are hiding and
waiting me...

# Extinct Memories

I found a box which was
Filled with the extincted memories.
I was looking to the box but
It was forbidden to open.

Undoubtedly that, that was my heart
Which filled with love, pain, hate
Happiness and yearning.

I was Pandora in my own story,
And the only hope is this box
Which filled with extincted memories.
They enjoined me not to open
And they told if I open
My all memories will extinct.
But I opened the box
Without hesitation and my
All memories spread to
The four winds.
Help me, mama!
Help me to remember!
Help me to remember our happiest times!
Please, mama!
Help me

LACHRYMOSE

to remember
my extincted memories…

# The Sunflower Garden or a Requiem for a Friend



You were wandering in sunflower heaven when I see you,
You were always my paradise, you were my sister.
Oh, my friend, do you hear my voice?
He took your soul, God, the Hunter.

Do you see the offerings I made for your healing?
What else should I do so you don't die?
Tell me, my little butterfly!
Your heart is like a compass.

You are my war, you are my victory,
This century is a century of pain and sorrow!
Ours is a sad story,
You were lying under a canopy.
And oh this me, I was weak!
No one is perfect, not even God!

LACHRYMOSE

Forgive me my friend!
May your soul reach heaven...
Goodbye forever...

# Birth of a Nightingale

A Nightingale was born
in the pitch black of night.
The mother of this Nightingale
sang peacefully day and night.
But that day
Her mother began to sing
the lament of eternal grief
with her delicate voice.
The birth of the Nightingale
was a harbinger of death
and grief, but the only
truth was she was cursed
by their master
they named God.
The Nightingale swore
not to sing peacefully
after her mother's
eternal grief.
The Nightingale had a
thicker and
more frightening
voice compared to
the others.
One day her mother

died suddenly and
the Nightingale started
to sing the Victory
March, which was
written by God with
the crimson blood
of her beloved mother.

# A Song of Gratitude for a Beloved Friend

I saw the light
of endurance to
exist in
this cruel world
in your eyes.

And the light was
as bright as
your merciful soul.

And I heard a song
of gratitude which
was written by
the dusts of my
infinite dreams.

Can you hear
the melody of
a song of gratitude
which's written
for you.

The sun

was getting
weaker than
we thought
but it is not
your fault.

Maybe you are
our sun,
Maybe you are
our sky.

Maybe you are
our light
of verity.
Maybe you are
our balance
of equality.

# V

# Delicate Heart of a Lover or Love Poems

*for the man who will be in my delicate heart forever*

# The Girl who wished to be Loved

I was that girl
Who wished to be loved.
Don't worry if I give you
The burnt daisies of my
Garden of Broken Hopes.
Don't be ashamed, if I
reveal my crush to you.
Because I loved you like a daughter
Who loved her father.

Don't reject me, if I ask you
to come near to you
Because I was lonely like
A Grim Reaper.
Because I was loveless like
My hopeless heart.
I was that girl
Who wished to be loved.
Don't worry, if I
Give you my desperate soul
Like a fallen woman who
Gave her maidenhood to
A mackerel.

# A Poem for My Beloved Man

Tell me, I'm not alone in all this,
Because you are my heaven in this hell.
I know you don't love me 'cause
I'm the big sinner, but give me
a chance to love you innocently.
surround my body with your being and
Tell me that You Love Me.

surround my body with your being and
Tell me that You Love Me.
Surround my soul with your love and
Tell me you never hated me.

You are my angel, my Heaven, my God,
I bow down before you and before your love, O my Lord!
I'm like a child without childhood,
O my Lord! Forgive me and my all sins!
Everything I did was for you!
O my Lord! Forgive me and my all sins!
Everything I did was for you!

I brought you white lilies from the Garden of the Virgin Mary but you
refused.
And I burned all those lilies with the

infinite fire of Hell.

# Light My Cigarette with the Spark of Your Love

Oh darlin', my darlin'
Light my cigarette with the
spark of your love,
Make my vision bright to
see you better with
my blind eyes.

Oh darlin', my darlin'!
What did you do to me?
Is that you Cupid, do you hear my voice?
Do you hear my cries for help?

Oh darlin', my darlin'
I'm in love with a *heartless* man!
I'm in love with a *relentless* man!

What's wrong with me?
Why is my heart beating like this?
Why is my heart pounding like this?

Oh darlin', my darlin'!
I reborn from the eternal ashes of

my extinguished cigarette!

Oh darlin', my darlin'!
What have I done?
Oh darlin', my darlin'!

# The Eyes Can Lie

Close your eyes and don't convince me to believe these lies,
But I want to look at your eyes because
I want to see you during lies my love.
Eyes can lie, but a heart and
a soul cannot lie.

Look at my heart and look at my soul,
you can't find what
let it be related to lies, my love.
But if you look carefully
you can see my loyalty to you!

# Hymn of Martyred Roses

It was the Hymn of Martyred Roses
like a painful cry which
offends every human being.
Only the dead or lovers could sing
this hymn which
was written with blood.

O Martyred Roses!
Tell me, who is the bravest
in this world?
Tell me, who is the bravest
in this love?

My heart was burning peacefully
in the scorching heat of love,
Can anyone hear my heart?
No, don't spill water! Don't!
I just want this love!
I want to burn to death for this love!

O Martyred Roses!
Tell me, which one of us
is more in love?
Tell me,one of us

LACHRYMOSE

was more lunatic?

It was the Hymn of Martyred Roses
like a painful cry which
offends every human being.
And I was singing
this hymn which
was written with blood.

# Seeds of Death

I was sure that
the seeds of
emotion sprouting in me
were not *love*.
It was just an *another* feeling
It was a *dark* feeling
like a *wish to die*.
It took root in
my delicate heart.

# He was a Holy Bird Who Sings

He was a holy bird who sings
the Hymn of Virgin Mary,
And I was that infidel,
Who killed him to shut him up.
And they punished me to
rewrite the Hymn of Virgin Mary
with my blood and breath.

# I Composed His Song of Mendaciousness

They asked me to write a song
for him and
I composed his
Song of Innocence.

They asked me to write a
sweet and charming song,
And I composed the
most sorrowful
song of innocence.

It might be a sweet
and cheering song,
but they were wrong,
I composed the most
poignant song of innocence.

Because he was cruel
like Lucifer
who owns the
entire Hell.

They asked and wanted me to be honest
to write a song

LACHRYMOSE

for him and
I composed his
Song of Mendaciousness.

# Untamed Heart

My heart is rough, wild
like a rind tiger!
Don't get too close to my heart,
it will hurt you like
you hurt me before.

O, my untamed heart,
How I will make you
listened to me?
O my untamed heart,
How I will make you
tamed?

These are the questions that hurt,
as if they were asked by you!
O, my untamed heart,
How I will make you
obey to me?

O, my untamed heart,
How I will make you
listened to me?
O my untamed heart,
How I will make you

as before?

O, my untamed, disobedient heart!
Can you hear me?
Can you hear my questions?
Can you hear the whispers
of my despair?

O, my untamed heart,
How I will make you
listened to me?
O my untamed heart,
How I will make you
as before?

# The Song of Fresh Almonds

I was singing the Song
of Fresh Almonds
on the top floor of a skyscraper
And I'm waiting for you to sing with me.

There is a hurricane in the middle
of my delicate heart
belongs only to you
and my heart was singing
the Song of Fresh Almonds.

# VI

# Satires for Manhood of Twenty First Century

*for all women in this world who have hope in their hearts*

# They Were Burying Their Innocent Women

They were burying
their innocent women
And they blindfolded them,
Instead of lamenting afterwards,
they were singing a song
of gratitude.

That's how humankind was,
they were relentless.
And their dead women were
just as delicate and pure.

This was the poem of
the innocent women
who lived in the
twenty-first century,
It was the poem of
the murdered women!

We were honoured to meet you,
hopes of the future!
It is up to you to understand us

and prevent them in the future.


Because *every* woman deserves
the love and respect she shows.
Because inside every woman lies
an innocent little *girl*
who owes her life
firstly to God and
then her *precious* family.

# A Satire for Manhood of Twenty First Century

Is it valiantness to kill innocent women
who never loved or obeyed you?
Is violence against women
describes virility?
But is it his stupidity that women
allow this to happen?

Women are like a flower that
no one wants to pick
because if you pick it, it loses its
root and becomes helpless.
Violence against women
is like picking a flower.

Because every woman is a *mother* with
the baby she carries in her womb.
Because every woman is a lover with
the lover she carries in her heart.
Remember, your mother
is also a woman,
a lover,
a hero.

# An Ode to all Women

Some of you are strong mothers,
some of you are strong women
walking step by step to *adulthood*!
But there is only one thing
that unites you all,
that all of us and all of us
are strong women.

Tell me that all this turmoil
and violence will end!
Tell me we will end all
this turmoil and violence!

We are strong women
We are the fruits from the
fertile womb of
our mothers!

Tell me that we will
dig the graves
of our murderers
with our innocent hands!

Tell me we will resurrect

and help all
our dead brethren to
rise from their graves!

Tell me, tell me!
Is the future as dark
for us as today?
Or will we be our
flambeau for
not finding our
own peace?

Tell me sibyl, tell me!
Tell me, what do your
eyes see?
What do you see
in our hands
where our destinies
are written?

# He Killed the Angel

He killed the Angel
who came to give him
some good news
from Heaven,
from our Father.

His dagger was covered
in the Angel's white blood.
The whiteness of the
angel's blood was
the color of a
woman's innocence.

He killed the Angel
who came to tell him
that he was accepted
into *her* Heaven.

He had no regrets
in rejecting her paradise
He didn't regret
killing the Angel
of Heaven,
of our Father.

# Epilogue

Dear reader, I am still madly in love with him. I still love him and I want him. But he's too blind and selfish to see that. And I'm naive and stupid enough to love him.